**MICROCOSM PUBLISHING** is Portland's most diversified publishing house and distributor with a focus on the colorful, authentic, and empowering. Our books and zines have put your power in your hands since 1996, equipping readers to make positive changes in their lives and in the world around them. Microcosm emphasizes skill-building, showing hidden histories, and fostering creativity through challenging conventional publishing wisdom with books and bookettes about DIY skills, food, bicycling, gender, self-care, and social justice. What was once a distro and record label was started by Joe Biel in his bedroom and has become among the oldest independent publishing houses in Portland, OR. We are a politically moderate, centrist publisher in a world that has inched to the right for the past 80 years.

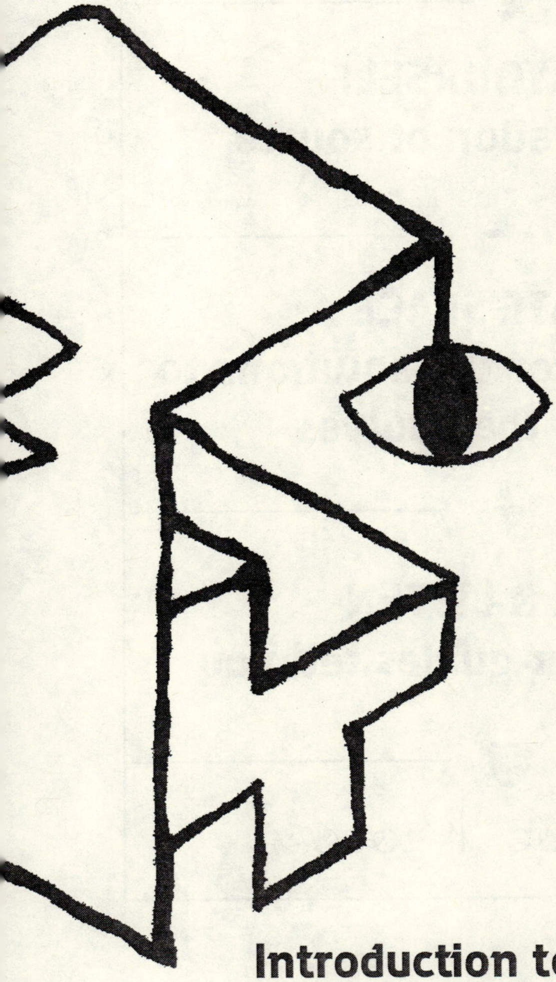

Introduction to

# Intuition & Clairvoyance

?

**TUNE YOURSELF**
**to the vibration of source**

**CREATE SPACE**
**in your mind for the solutions to present themselves**

**LOOK & LISTEN**
**for what your guides tell you**

*Intuitive Process*

## Introduction

Life is always giving us guidance. We can learn to listen to and look for the cues shared with us. There is no answer we don't already have within.

Accessing your knowledge of non-physical reality takes practice and an open mind. We must be willing to hear new ideas and see new pathways. This booklet will help you hone your psychic abilities with simple exercises that encourage you to listen to the source within you, and recognize signs from the world outside of you.

The first five exercises are designed to help you listen to the non-physical energy within you. The answers you're looking for can come in a voice in your head, or a vision in your mind's eye.

The last two exercises help you train your mind to look for signs in your physical world. What you notice, you get more of, and what you focus on expands. Train your attention to focus on that which you want and what you want more of and it has no choice but to present itself to you.

## Meditation for Becoming a Match to the Solution

Breathe in and raise your vibration!
Breathe out and release your resistance

Breathe in and raise your vibration!
Breathe out and release your resistance

Relax and know that any problem you have,
has already created the solution.

Breathe in and say thank you for the problem
Breathe out and relax into this moment

Breathe in and open your mind
Breathe out and be here now

Your solution is created the moment you become aware of the problem. Allow yourself to relax into this moment, where you can become a match to the solution right now.

Breathe in and recognize your contrast
Breathe out and remember your contrast creates

Every time you experience something you don't want, it creates what you do want. Your contrast is just a means of getting what you want.

Breathe in and acknowledge your contrast
Breathe out and ask yourself, "What is it that I would prefer?"

Relax and let yourself be whole right now. Regardless of your problems, or solutions, you are whole and complete right now and you don't need anything to feel good. You can choose to feel good right now, regardless of your circumstances.

Breathe in and feel good about yourself. You've come so far!
Breathe out and say thank you for this moment

Thank your body for bringing you along this far. Thank the universe or god or infinite intelligence for this experience. Thank yourself for choosing to be in this present moment.

Breathe in and feel yourself becoming a match to the solution
Breathe out and relax your body

Imagine how you'll feel when you get this solution. Imagine feeling extreme relief, that feeling of a huge weight being lifted from your shoulders. Imagine you feel like a cork, being held under water, suddenly allowed to bob to surface.

Breathe in and decide how you want to feel when you get your solution
Breathe out and know you can have that feeling right now

Whatever your problem is, you don't need the solution to be happy. You don't need to receive that thing you want to be happy. You can choose to feel as good as you would if you had the solution right now.

Breathe in and say "I don't care if I ever get the solution! I can be happy right now!" Breathe out and relax your body. You're becoming a match to the solution right now.

Breathe in and practice feeling how you'd feel if you received your solution. Breathe out and milk that feeling.

Allow yourself to feel that feeling of relief, of tears of joy because life really does love you and it really is working out. It was fine, it all worked out, you're doing such a good job!

Breathe in and remember life does love you
Breathe out and know you are one with life

Breathe in and feel better already
Breathe out and feel relief

Allow yourself to feel those tears of joy. Your problem is solved. It all worked out. You didn't have to lift a finger. The magick of life took care of everything for you. You already were in the right place at the right time and you already were doing everything right. Your only work is to relax and enjoy right now because you can be happy regardless of your circumstances. When you stop caring about getting the solution to your problem, you'll see it's already inside of you.

1

# What's Your Solution?

Life exists in waves. Every aspect of life has an opposite and that is why we are able to experience both. Without one, there cannot be the other. With every problem exists a solution. Awareness of the solution is a matter of focus. When we are overcome by a problem, it can be difficult to see a solution. It can be difficult to even believe in its existence.

Sometimes, we have to just stop looking for the solution. But at the same time, stop looking at the problem.

Write down your problem in the space indicated. How does your problem make you feel? Circle it. Now find the opposite, positive emotion and circle it. That is the feeling that your problem is causing you to ask for. List 6 things that make you feel that way in the space provided.

Now forget about your problem. Forget about the solution. Focus on the feeling. If you find yourself thinking about the problem, say to yourself, "I've decided to feel good about that. It's working itself out." Then remember an item on your list and feel your desired feeling. When you've forgotten the problem, the solution will present itself.

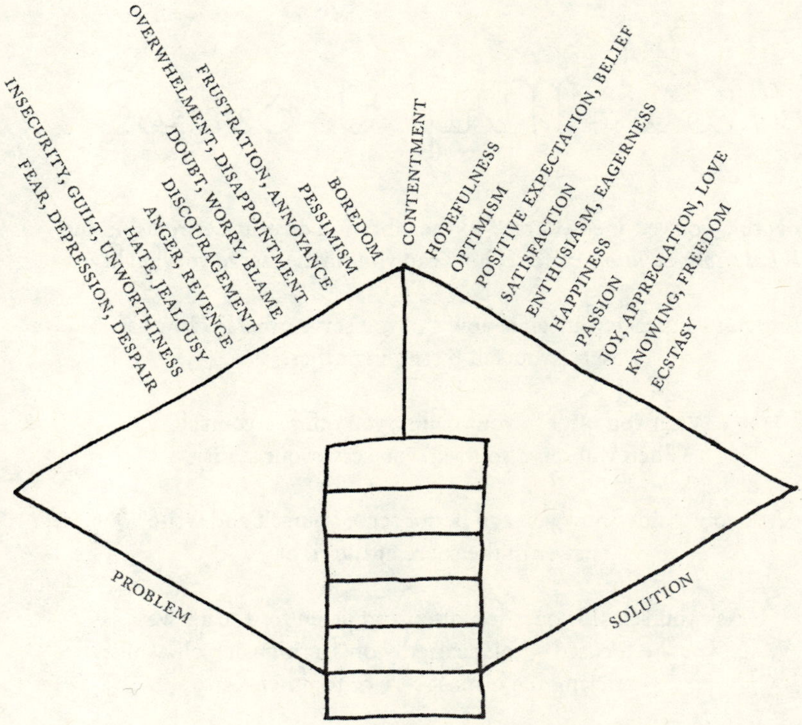
INSECURITY, GUILT, UNWORTHINESS
FEAR, DEPRESSION, DESPAIR
HATE, JEALOUSY
ANGER, REVENGE
DISCOURAGEMENT
DOUBT, WORRY, BLAME
OVERWHELMENT, DISAPPOINTMENT
FRUSTRATION, ANNOYANCE
PESSIMISM
BOREDOM
CONTENTMENT
HOPEFULNESS
OPTIMISM
POSITIVE EXPECTATION, BELIEF
SATISFACTION
ENTHUSIASM, EAGERNESS
HAPPINESS
PASSION
JOY, APPRECIATION, LOVE
KNOWING, FREEDOM
ECSTASY
PROBLEM
SOLUTION

2

# How May I Serve?

Now that you've tuned yourself to the vibration of your desire using the *What's Your Solution* exercise, how can you further serve your reality?

How can you serve yourself? How can you serve others? How can you serve yourself by serving others?

What you offer to your reality, you offer to yourself.
When you serve yourself, you serve your reality.

Ask your guides how you can better serve yourself and write your answer in the space at the right.

Ask yourself this question often and listen for the answer.
When you are focused wholeheartedly on serving yourself, you are offering the utmost service to others.

This focus creates space for the universe to fill in the rest.

# Ask the Universe Anything

Go ahead, ask.

Do you believe the universe provides? Do you believe the answer is always right there winking at you, waiting for you to pay her some attention?

Of course you do. Not only do you believe, you know.

*Ask the Universe Anything* then trace the labyrinth while you listen for the answer.

**Question:**

________________________________________

Trace the labyrinth back out while you allow yourself to take its advice.

**Answer:**

________________________________________

4

# Non-dominant Hand

Your body is a fractal of the universe, and as such, it holds all the answers. The hand you use to write with is filled with logic and understanding, but have you ever tried drawing or writing with your non-dominant hand? Using your "other" hand to draw or write can unleash a world of answers and creativity you didn't know you had inside of you.

In the space below, use your dominant hand to write down a question you'd like the answer to. Then, switch to your non-dominant hand and let the answer flow.

**Question:** ______________________________________

**Answer:** ______________________________________

On the page to the right, draw a picture using your non-dominant hand. Try asking yourself one of the following questions, and see what your hand creates.

WHAT DOES MY HIGHEST SELF LOOK LIKE?

WHAT SHOULD I FOCUS MY ENERGY ON?

WHAT MIGHT HAPPEN ON THE BEST DAY OF MY LIFE?

WHO AM I?

HOW CAN I RELAX AND ENJOY THE MOMENT?

WHAT DO I NEED TO LET GO OF?

5

# Your Own Medicine

In each of the numbered potions on the right, write a piece of advice that you've heard yourself give someone else.

If your reality reflects you, and everything in your reality is a reflection of the signal you send, then the same is true for the people with whom you share this co-creative experience. Each person in your reality can only reflect your current beliefs about your reality.

When you hear yourself giving advice, remember it is only yourself you are talking to. Think someone could change the way she is living her life? The way you see her situation is only a reflection of your beliefs. You are noticing your own perceived short-comings.

Listen to what you are telling others to do and remember that you are only your higher self talking to reflections of yourself.

Then, take your own advice.

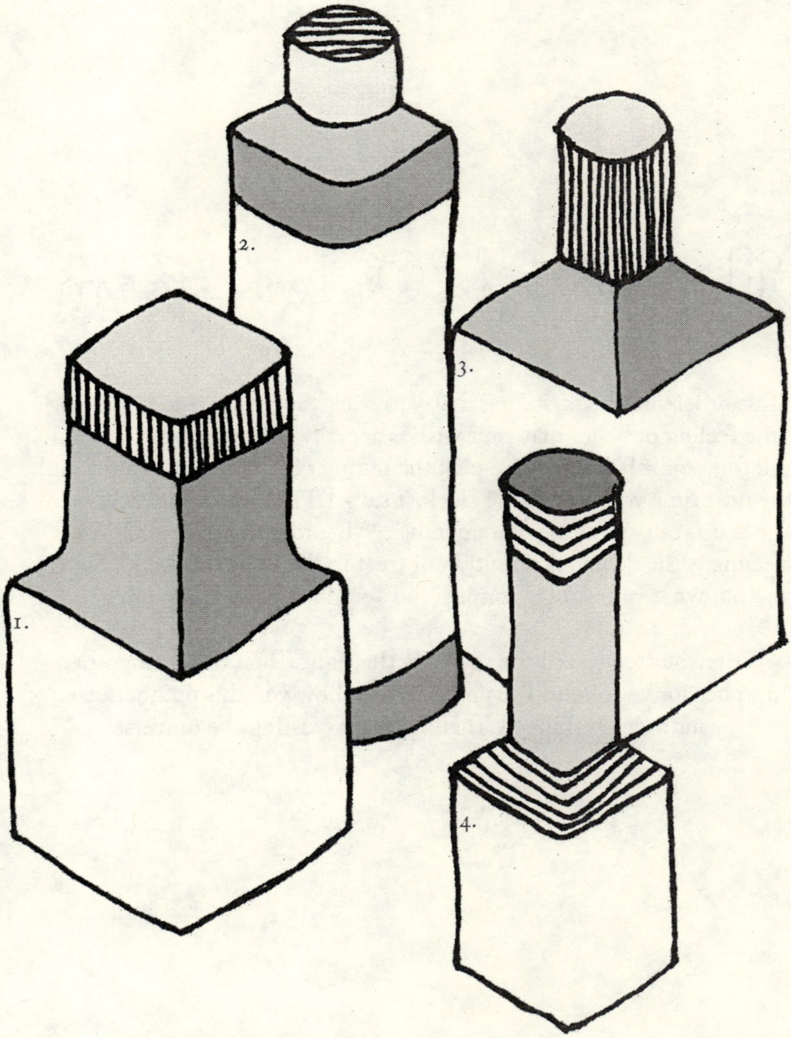


1. Friend 2. Colleague 3. Society 4. Family Member

6

# Universal Order Form

This order-number system is a way to trick your mind into practicing the feeling of belief that your wish is actually being granted. Say you ask for a milkshake, and you pick the number 33. An hour goes by and the next time you look at the clock, it says 4:33. A quiver of excitement goes up your spine, as you remember, "My order number is 33!" That feeling is the delicious sensation of trust in the universe, the knowing that what you want is coming and you don't have to lift a finger.

Write your request in the space on the right. Then choose an order number for your item. The universe will show you this number when your order is shipped. Thank you for trusting the universe!

ORDER #

7

# Scavenger Hunt

When you look for something, you find more of it.
When you get your mind in the practice of looking for what you want, you'll notice that you see it more frequently.

Look for evidence of each of the items on the right and describe it in the space provided.

Notice how when you look for something, you see it more and more? That principle can be applied to any aspect of your life.

1. Hidden Treasure
2. Magick
3. Synchronicity
4. Hilarity
5. Well Being
6. Health
7. Love
8. Alien Activity
9. Effortlessness

# INTRODUCTION TO INTUITION AND CLAIRVOYANCE

Jessica Mullen and Kelly Cree

ISBN 9781621062417

This is Microcosm #612

First Published 2018



For a catalog, write or visit:

Microcosm Publishing

2752 N Williams Ave.

Portland, OR 97227

**www.Microcosm.Pub**

**To join the ranks of high-class stores that feature Microcosm titles, talk to your rep:** In the U.S. **Como** (Atlantic), **Fujii** (Midwest), **Book Travelers West** (Pacific), **Turnaround** in Europe, **Manda/UTP** in Canada, **New South** in Australia, and **GPS** in Asia, India, Africa, and South America.

If you bought this on Amazon, I'm so sorry because you could have gotten it cheaper and supported a small, independent publisher at www.**Microcosm.Pub**

Global labor conditions are bad, and our roots in industrial Cleveland in the 70s and 80s made us appreciate the need to treat workers right. Therefore, our books are MADE IN THE USA and printed on post-consumer paper.